# Tiny Hearts
## with
# *Big Feelings*

Preschoolers letters to their parents

# EWURAMMA

**TINY HEARTS WITH BIG FEELINGS: PRESCHOOLERS LETTERS TO THEIR PARENTS**

Copyright © 2024 by Ewuramma
All rights reserved.

ISBN: 978-0-9849805-8-1

Copyright © 2024 Our Paraclete. All rights reserved.

**Published by:** Our Paraclete, an imprint of Our Paraclete Publishers.

All rights reserved. No part of this book may be reproduced or transmitted in any form or by any means, electronic or mechanical, including photocopying, recording, or by any information storage and retrieval system, without permission in writing from the publisher.

**Contact Author on:**
ourparacletefoundation.inc@gmail.com

**Designed by:**
Indes Procom Limited.
info@indesprocom.com
www.indesprocom.com

## CONTENTS

Dedication   4
Preface   4
Prelude   4
Apologia   5
Foreword   6

1. AN AUTHORITATIVE PARENT   7
2. AN AUTHORITARIAN PARENT   20
3. PERMISSIVE PARENT   32
4. UNINVOLVED PARENT   45
5. SAYING NO TO A CHILD   56
6. EFFECTIVELY PUNISHING A CHILD   62

Conclusion   71
Acknowledgments   72
Welcome to our Paraclete Family!!   73
Email us your story!!!   74
Bibliography   75

# DEDICATION

This book is dedicated to all parents who strive to understand and connect with their children on a deeper level. To the children who shared their feelings and thoughts through these letters, your honesty and innocence are truly inspiring. And to you, the reader, for embarking on this journey of understanding and growth with us. This book is for you.

# PREFACE

This book is a collection of heartfelt letters from preschoolers to their parents. It's a window into the innocent minds of children, their emotions, feelings, and perceptions of their parents' styles. It's a testament to the profound impact parenting styles have on a child's development. The book aims to shed light on the importance of understanding and adapting parenting styles to foster a healthy parent-child relationship.

# PRELUDE

Before we delve into the heart of this book, let's take a moment to appreciate the purity and honesty of a child's perspective. These letters are not just words on a page but echoes of their thoughts, feelings, and experiences. They reflect the children's understanding of their world and their place in it. As you read these letters, you may find insights into your own parenting style and how it impacts your child.

# APOLOGIA

In crafting this book, my intention was to provide a platform for the voices of preschoolers, often overlooked in discussions about parenting styles. These letters are not for blaming or condemning but for revealing how parenting styles affect the child's point of view.

The emotions and feelings expressed by these young children are raw and unfiltered, providing a unique insight into their world. While the letters may sometimes seem simplistic or naive, they reflect the genuine experiences and perceptions of these children.

The responses from the parents are not intended to endorse or condemn any particular parenting style. Instead, they serve to illustrate the potential effects of different parenting styles on children. They aim to stimulate thinking and help parents examine their own ways of parenting.

This book is not a manual or guide to parenting. It does not claim to have all the answers. Instead, it is an invitation to dialogue, a spark for more profound thinking and conversation about the intricate and difficult responsibility of raising children.

I understand that every parent-child relationship is unique and that what works for one may not work for another. My hope is that this book will inspire parents to listen more closely to their children, to understand their feelings and needs, and to adapt their parenting style in a way that best supports their child's development.

In conclusion, I offer this book as a humble contribution to the ongoing conversation about parenting. I hope it serves as a valuable resource for parents and a testament to the profound impact they have on their children's lives. I welcome all feedback and criticism, as they provide opportunities for growth and improvement. Thank you for taking the time to engage with this work.

Ewuramma Hannah Boah

# FOREWORD

In the pages that follow, you will find a collection of heartfelt letters from preschoolers to their parents. These letters, in their innocence and honesty, offer a rare glimpse into the minds of children, their emotions, feelings, and perceptions of their parents' styles.

Parenting is a journey of happiness, difficulties, education, and development. It is a journey that shapes not only the lives of our children but also our own. As parents, we strive to understand our children, to connect with them on a deeper level, and to guide them as they navigate their way in the world.

This book is a testament to that journey. It shows how parenting styles affect a child's growth and highlights the need to know and adjust these styles to promote a good parent-child relationship.

The letters contained within these pages are not just words on a page but echoes of the thoughts, feelings, and experiences of our children. They reflect their understanding of their world and their place in it. As you read these letters, you may find insights into your own parenting style and how it impacts your child.

This book is not a manual or guide to parenting. It does not claim to have all the answers. Instead, it sparks conversation, a way to think and talk more deeply about the complicated and hard job of parenting.

As you embark on this journey through the pages of this book, it may inspire you to listen more closely to your children, to understand their feelings and needs, and to adapt your parenting style in a way that best supports their development.

Thank you for taking the time to engage with this work. I hope it serves as a valuable resource for you and a testament to the profound impact you have on your children's lives.

Enjoy the journey.

**Miss Lois Owusu**
A mother of two boys and a teenage girl

# AN AUTHORITATIVE PARENT

An authoritative parent is like a loving teacher. They make rules, like when it's time for bed or when we need to eat our veggies because they want us to be healthy and safe. But they also listen to us, understand how we feel, and are always there to help when things are tough.

They give us big hugs, play with us, and let us learn things on our own, too!

# LETTER TO AN AUTHORITATIVE DAD

Dear Daddy,

Please, you are my superhero! You make me laugh with your funny faces and tickles. I love it when we build towers with my blocks, and you let me knock them down.

Thank you for carrying me on your shoulders so I can see the world so big. I feel like I can touch the sky!

You teach me to be brave and strong, like when I'm scared of the dark. You say it's okay and that you're right there. That makes me feel better.

I love you more than the biggest dinosaur. You're the best daddy in the whole wide world!

Biggest hug and a high five,

Little One

# RESPONSE FROM AN AUTHOURITATIVE DAD

Dear Little One's Name,

Your letter made my day! I'm so glad to be your superhero. Your laughter is my ` sound, and I love building towers with you and watching you knock them down.

I'm happy to carry you on my shoulders and show you the big, beautiful world. And please remember, even when the sky seems out of reach, I'll always be there to lift you up.

I'm proud of you for being brave and strong, even when you're scared of the dark. Please remember, it's okay to be scared sometimes, and I'll always be there to make you feel better.

Your love means more to me than the biggest dinosaur in the world.
You are the best little one a daddy could ever ask for!

Biggest hug and a high five back,

Daddy

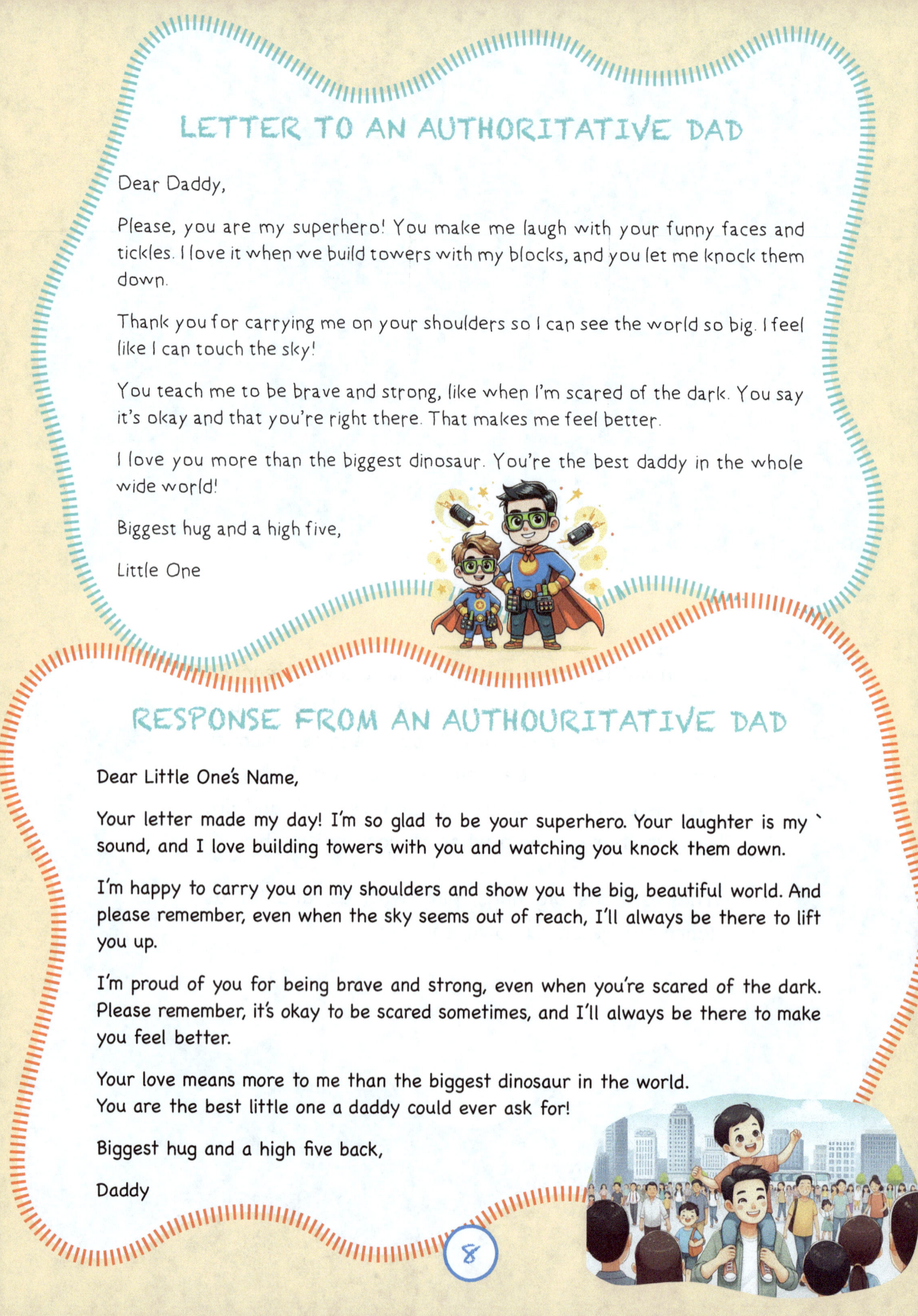

# LETTER TO AN AUTHORITATIVE MOM

Dear Mommy,

Please, thank you for being my mommy. You give me the best hugs and make me feel safe. I like it when you read stories to me and tuck me in at night.

You make yummy food, and you know just what to do when I feel yucky. You kiss my boo-boos and make them better.

I love you more than all the stars and all the toys in the world. You are the best mommy ever!

Big hugs and kisses,

Your Little One

# RESPONSE FROM AN AUTHOURITATIVE MOM

Dear Little One,

Your letter filled my heart with so much joy! I'm so glad to be your mommy. Your hugs are the best part of my day, and I love reading stories to you and tucking you in at night.

I'm happy to hear that you enjoy the food I make for you, and please I'll always be here to make you feel better when you're feeling yucky.
Your boo-boos are safe with my kisses!

Your love means more to me than all the stars in the sky and all the toys in the world. You are the best little one a mommy could ever ask for!

Big hugs and kisses back,

Mommy

# LETTER TO AN AUTHORITATIVE DAD

Dear Daddy,

Please, I love you more than a dinosaur! You are the superest because you let me do super fun stuff. I can zoom in on my race cars before sleepy time and stay up late to see the moon. You say yes lots, and that makes me super happy!

Sometimes, I get a teensy bit scared when I'm not sure what to do, like when I have too many teddies to play with. But you give me cool high fives and fist bumps, and then I feel super brave.

Daddy, you are like a big, strong robot, very tough and kind. I like it when we play and make robot noises together. You don't get grumpy when I scatter my toy soldiers, and that's super fun!

Can we please have a battle with my toy soldiers tomorrow? I want to command them like you do and pretend they are superheroes, but I will share with you too, because you are my favorite daddy.

Thank you for being so kind and letting me have fun. I love you more than all the racing cars in the world!

High fives and robot noises,

Your Little Boy

# RESPONSE FROM AN AUTHOURITATIVE DAD

Dear My Little Boy,

Your letter made my day super bright! I'm super happy to hear how much you love our special times together, from our late-night moon-watching to our fun toy soldier battles. Your joy is my super joy.

I understand that having lots of teddies to choose from can sometimes be a little tricky. Please remember, I'm always here to help you pick. And it's totally okay to scatter your toy soldiers - it's all part of the fun!

A battle with your toy soldiers sounds like a super idea! We can command them and pretend they are superheroes, just like you suggested. I can't wait!

Thank you for your sweet words and for being such a super son. I love you more than all the racing cars in the world!

With all my love,

Daddy

# LETTER TO AN AUTHORITATIVE MOM

Dear Mommy,

I love you lots and lots! Please, you are the best because you let me do lots of things. I can eat cookies before dinner and stay up late to watch the stars. You say yes a lot, and that makes me happy!

Sometimes, I get a little scared when I don't know what I should do, like when I have too many toys to choose from. But you give me hugs and kisses, and then I feel better.

Mommy, you are like a soft pillow, very squishy and nice. I like it when we play and laugh together. You don't get mad when I make a mess with my paintings, and that's fun!

Please can we have a tea party with my dolls tomorrow? I want to pour the tea as you do and give them cookies, but I will share with you, too, because you are my favorite mommy.

Thank you for being so nice and letting me do things. I love you more than all the stars in the sky!

Hugs and butterfly kisses,

Your Little Girl

# RESPONSE FROM AN AUTHOURITATIVE MOM

Dear My Little Girl,

Your letter filled my day with joy! I'm thrilled to hear how much you enjoy our special moments together, from our late-night stargazing to our fun painting sessions. Your happiness is my happiness.

I understand that having too many choices can sometimes be overwhelming. Please remember, I'm always here to help you decide. And it's okay to make a mess with your paintings - it's all part of the creative process!

A tea party with your dolls sounds like a wonderful idea! Please we can pour the tea and share cookies, just like you suggested. I'm looking forward to it.

Thank you for your sweet words and for being such a wonderful daughter. I love you more than all the stars in the sky!

With all my love,

Mommy

## LETTER TO AN AUTHORITATIVE DAD

Dear Daddy,

I love it when we play games together. You always let me win, and that makes me feel happy. But I heard Mommy saying that it's good to learn to lose sometimes, too. Please can we try that? I want to learn to be a good sport, just like you.

And Daddy, can we do more puzzles together? You make them seem so easy, and I learn so much. It's my favorite time with you.

You're the best daddy in the whole wide world!

Love and giggles,

Your Little Boy

## RESPONSE FROM AN AUTHOURITATIVE DAD

Dear Little Boy ,

Your letter made me so happy! I'm proud of you for wanting to learn about being a good sport. It's an important part of playing games, and I'm glad you're ready to learn.

Please, we can definitely do more puzzles together. I enjoy our puzzle time, too, and I'm glad to hear it's your favorite.

Thank you for your kind words. You're the best son a daddy could ever wish for!

Love and giggles back,

Daddy

# LETTER TO AN AUTHORITATIVE MOM

Dear Mommy,

I love it when we bake cookies! You let me put in the chocolate chips, and that's super fun. Daddy says we should clean up too. Can we please do that next time? I want to be good like you.

And Mommy, can we read more books? When you read, it's like a fairy tale. It's my favorite time with you.

You're the best mommy in the whole wide world!

Hugs and tickles,

Your Little Girl

# RESPONSE FROM AN AUTHOURITATIVE MOM

Dear Mary,

Your letter made my heart dance! I'm so proud of you for wanting to learn to clean up. That's a big part of baking cookies, and I'm excited you want to try it.

Yes, please, we can definitely read more books together. I love our story time, too, and I'm thrilled it's your favorite.

Thank you for your sweet words. You're the most wonderful daughter a mommy could ever dream of!

Hugs and tickles back,

Mommy

# BALANCED VS. UNBALANCED PARENTING: CONTRASTING CHILD OUTCOMES

Children raised by Authoritative parents, like the ones described in the letters, tend to grow up to be well-adjusted individuals who are capable, happy, and successful.

## POSITIVE OUTCOMES

**Self-confidence:** They believe in their abilities to learn new things.

**Good social skills:** They are able to interact effectively and harmoniously with others.

**Emotional control and regulation:** They can manage and express their emotions in a healthy way.

**Happier dispositions:** They generally have a positive outlook on life.

**Creativity:** They are able to think outside the box and come up with unique ideas.

**Motivation:** They have the drive to achieve their goals.

**Future career success:** They are more likely to prosper and achieve success in their careers as adults.

These children are also more likely to be resilient, able to handle losses and solve problems effectively. They learn from their mistakes, as authoritative parents allow their children to make mistakes and support them through the learning process.

In society, these individuals are likely to contribute positively due to their problem-solving skills, creativity, and ability to work well with others. They are likely to be responsible citizens who respect rules and boundaries while also valuing independence and personal growth.

## NEGATIVE OUTCOMES

While the authoritative style is generally associated with positive outcomes, it's important to note that no parenting style is perfect, and negative outcomes can occur. These may include:

**Pressure and Stress:** Children may feel pressure to meet the high expectations set by their parents, leading to stress and anxiety.

**Over-dependence on external validation:** Some children may become overly reliant on external validation and praise, struggling to develop intrinsic motivation.

**Difficulty with failure:** Because authoritative parents often foster an environment where success is celebrated, some children may have a hard time coping with failure.

**Less risk-taking:** Some children may be less likely to take risks or explore new things due to fear of disappointing their parents.

To balance the child's outcomes and ensure they grow up to be wonderful and beneficial to humanity and society, parents practicing an authoritative style could consider incorporating elements of the permissive parenting style. Here are some steps they can take:

**Encourage Open Expression:** Permissive parents often encourage open expression of feelings. Authoritative parents can create this by providing an environment where children can share their feelings openly.

**Promote Flexibility:** Permissive parents are often flexible and adaptable. Authoritative parents can incorporate this by being flexible with rules and expectations when appropriate, teaching children that adaptability is a valuable life skill.

**Nurture Creativity:** Permissive parents often allow children to explore their interests freely, fostering creativity and independent thinking. Authoritative parents can nurture this by providing opportunities for creative exploration.

**Validate Feelings:** Permissive parents often validate their children's feelings. Authoritative parents can adopt this by acknowledging their children's feelings and letting them know it's okay to feel the way they do.

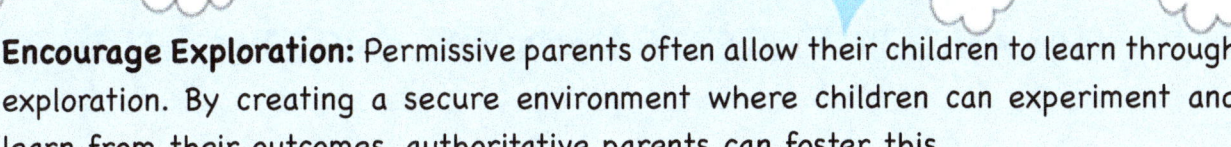

**Encourage Exploration:** Permissive parents often allow their children to learn through exploration. By creating a secure environment where children can experiment and learn from their outcomes, authoritative parents can foster this.

**Promote Self-Expression:** Permissive parents often allow children to express themselves freely, whether it's through their clothing, hobbies, or in their choices. Authoritative parents can adopt this by encouraging children to express their individuality and respecting their choices.

**Encourage Balance:** While permissive parents can sometimes be seen as too lenient, they often promote a sense of balance in their children's lives. Authoritative parents can learn from this by ensuring there's a balance between discipline and freedom.

**Provide Unconditional Support:** Permissive parents are often very supportive and forgiving. Authoritative parents can incorporate this by providing unconditional support and love, showing their children that they'll be there for them, no matter what.

Remember, every child is unique, and what works for one might not work for another. Parents should adjust their parenting methods to suit the specific needs of their children. It's also important to note that parenting is a journey, and it's okay to make mistakes along the way. The key is to learn from these mistakes and continue to strive to be the best parent you can be.

# A BALANCED PARENT AND BALANCED CHILD

## LETTER FROM A FOUR-YEAR-OLD TO A PREVIOUSLY AUTHORITATIVE BUT NOW BALANCED DAD

Dear Daddy,

Please, remember when you used to always win our games. But now, you let me win sometimes, and that's so fun! I feel like a big kid winning like you. And now, we do more puzzles together too. You make them seem so easy, and I learn so much. It's my favorite time with you. You're the best daddy in the whole wide world!

Love and giggles,

Bob

## RESPONSE FROM A PREVIOUSLY AUTHORITATIVE BUT NOW BALANCED DAD

Dear Bob,

Your letter made my day! I'm proud of you for wanting to learn about being a good sport. It's an important part of playing games, and I'm glad you're ready to learn. Please, we can definitely do more puzzles together. I enjoy our puzzle time too, and I'm glad to hear it's your favorite. Thank you for your kind words. You're the best son a daddy could ever wish for!

Love and giggles back,

Daddy

## LETTER FROM A FOUR-YEAR-OLD TO A PREVIOUSLY AUTHORITATIVE BUT NOW BALANCED MOM

Dear Mommy,

Please, I remember when we used to bake cookies, and I would just watch. But now, you let me put in the chocolate chips, and that's super fun! I feel like a big kid baking like you. And now, we read more books together too. When you read, it's like a fairy tale. It's my favorite time with you. You're the best mommy in the whole wide world!

Hugs and tickles,

Mary

## RESPONSE FROM A PREVIOUSLY AUTHORITATIVE BUT NOW BALANCED MOM

Dear Mary,

Your letter made my heart dance! I'm so proud of you for wanting to learn to bake. That's a big part of making cookies, and I'm excited you want to try it. Please, we can definitely read more books together. I love our story time too, and I'm thrilled it's your favorite. Thank you for your sweet words. You're the most wonderful [son/daughter] a mommy could ever dream of!

Hugs and tickles back,

Mommy

# AN AUTHORITARIAN PARENT

Authoritarian Parent: An authoritarian parent is like a strict captain of a ship. They make all the rules and expect you to follow them without question, just like a captain expects his crew to follow orders. They want to keep the ship running smoothly, but sometimes, it might feel like they're being too bossy.

## LETTER TO AN AUTHOURITARIAN DAD

Dear Daddy,

Please, you always give me the biggest piece of cake, and that makes me feel special. But I heard Mommy saying that it's good to learn to share too. Please can we try that? I want to learn to be generous, just like you.

And Daddy, can we bake more cookies together? You make the yummiest cookies, and I learn so much. It's my favorite time with you.

You're the best daddy in the whole wide world!

Love and cookie crumbs,

Little One

## RESPONSE FROM AN AUTHOURITARIAN DAD

Dear Little One,

Your letter has been noted. It's important to understand that sharing is a crucial part of life. We will certainly work on that. It's not just about wanting to learn; it's about implementing it in your actions.

As for baking more cookies, we can schedule that when it's appropriate. Please remember everything should be done in moderation.

Thank you for your words. Please remember being the best daughter involves listening, learning, and improving.

Regards,

Daddy

## LETTER TO AN AUTHOURITARIAN MOM

Dear Mommy,

I love it when we blow bubbles! You let me hold the wand, and that's super fun. But Daddy says we should not spill the soap. Can we please try that next time? I want to be careful like you. And Mommy, can we read more animal stories together?

You make the stories so fun, and I learn lots. It's my best time with you. You're the best mommy ever!

Hugs and bubbles,

Your Little One

## RESPONSE FROM AN AUTHOURITARIAN MOM

Dear Little One,

Your letter made me smile! I'm glad you want to learn not to spill soap. That's a part of blowing bubbles, and I'm happy you want to try it. Please, we can definitely read more animal stories together. I love our story time too, and I'm glad it's your favorite.

Thank you for your sweet words. You're the best daughter a mommy could ever wish for!

Hugs and bubbles back,

Mommy

## LETTER TO AN AUTHOURITARIAN DAD

Dear Daddy,

Please you always let me ride the tallest slide at the park, and that makes me feel brave. But I heard Mommy saying that it's good to learn to be careful too. Please can we try that? I want to learn to be safe, just like you.

And Daddy, can we build more sandcastles together?
You make the tallest towers, and I learn so much.
It's my favorite time with you.

You're the bravest daddy in the whole wide world!

Love and sandcastles,

Your Little One

## RESPONSE FROM AN AUTHOURITARIAN DAD

Dear Little One,

Your letter has been noted. It's important to understand that being careful is a crucial part of life. We will certainly work on that. It's not just about wanting to learn; it's about implementing it in your actions.

As for building more sandcastles, we can schedule that when it's appropriate. Please remember everything should be done in moderation.

Thank you for your words. Remember, being the best son involves listening, learning, and improving.

Regards,

Daddy

## LETTER TO AN AUTHOURITARIAN MOM

Dear Mommy,

I love it when we play with playdough! You let me make fun shapes, and that's super fun. But Daddy says we should put the playdough away too. Please, can we do that next time? I want to be neat and tidy like you. And Mommy, can we read more fairy tales together?

You make the stories so fun, and I learn lots. It's my best time with you. You're the best mommy ever!

Hugs and playdough shapes,

Your Little Boy

## RESPONSE FROM AN AUTHOURITARIAN MOM

Dear Little One,

Your letter made me smile! I'm glad you want to learn to put things away. That's a part of playing with playdough, and I'm happy you want to try. Please, we can definitely read more fairy tales together. I love our story time too, and I'm glad it's your favorite.

Thank you for your sweet words. You're the best son a mommy could ever wish for!

Hugs and playdough shapes back,

Mommy

# LETTER TO AN AUTHOURITARIAN DAD

Dear Daddy,

I've been studying really hard every day, even till late. I feel like I'm growing up so fast! But sometimes, I hear Mommy say that it's good to go to bed early. Can we try that this weekend? I want to learn to be disciplined, just like you.

And Daddy, this weekend, instead of studying, can we play? Mommy always says, "All work and no play makes Jack a dull boy." I think she's right. I would love to spend some time playing and having fun.

Also, can we read more adventure stories together? You make the stories come alive and I learn so much from them. It's my favorite time with you.

You're the best daddy in the whole wide world! Can I have a little break this weekend, please?

Love,

Your Little One

# RESPONSE FROM AN AUTHOURITARIAN DAD

Dear Your Little One

I appreciate your letter and understand your feelings. It's important to remember that discipline and routine are crucial parts of life, and going to bed early is a part of that. We will certainly work on implementing this.

As for taking a break and playing, I understand the importance of balance. However, everything should be done in moderation. We can certainly schedule some time for play and reading more adventure stories together when it's appropriate.

Remember, being the best involves listening, learning, and improving. I'm proud of you for expressing your feelings and thoughts. Let's continue to work together on this journey.

Best regards,

Daddy

# LETTER TO AN AUTHOURITARIAN MOM

Dear Mommy,

I love it when we plant flowers in the garden! You let me hold the watering can, and that's super fun. But Daddy says we should not overwater the plants. Can we please try that next time? I want to be careful like you. And Mommy, can we watch more animal movies together on our movie nights?

You make the movie nights so fun, and I learn lots. It's my best time with you. You're the best mommy ever!

Hugs and popcorn,

Your Little One

# RESPONSE FROM AN AUTHOURITARIAN MOM

Dear Your Little One

Your letter made me smile! I'm glad you want to learn not to overwater the plants. That's a part of gardening, and I'm happy you want to try it. Yes, please, we can definitely watch more animal movies together on our movie nights.

I love our movie nights too, and I'm glad it's your favorite. Thank you for your sweet words. You're the best [son/daughter] a mommy could ever wish for!

Hugs and popcorn back,

Mommy

# BALANCED VS. UNBALANCED PARENTING: CONTRASTING CHILD OUTCOMES

Children raised by Authoritarian parents, like the ones described in the letters, may exhibit the following characteristics in society:

## POSITIVE OUTCOMES

**Discipline:** These children often learn to follow rules and exhibit disciplined behavior.

**Respect for Authority:** They may develop a strong respect for authority and tend to follow societal norms.

**Academic Success:** Some studies suggest that these children may perform well academically due to the high expectations set by their parents.

## NEGATIVE OUTCOMES

**Low Self-Esteem:** They may have lower self-esteem as they may feel that they can never meet their parents' high standards.

**Poor Social Skills:** They may have difficulties in social interactions as they may not have been allowed to interact freely with their peers during their childhood.

**Dependence:** They may rely heavily on others for decision-making as they were not encouraged to think independently during their childhood.

Aggression: They may exhibit aggressive behavior, including bullying.

**Mental Health Problems:** They may be more susceptible to mental health issues like depression.

To balance the outcomes and ensure the child grows up to be wonderful and beneficial to humanity and society, parents practicing an authoritarian style could consider incorporating elements of other parenting styles, such as authoritative parenting. Here are some steps they can take:

**Encourage Open Communication:** Authoritarian parents often have a "because I said so" approach. Instead, they could encourage open communication, explain their reasoning, and listen to the child's perspective.

**Promote Independence:** Rather than making all decisions for the child, parents could allow the child to make age-appropriate decisions. This can help the child develop independence and decision-making skills.

**Balance Expectations:** While it's important to have high expectations, parents should also ensure they are realistic and achievable. This can help boost the child's self-esteem.

**Foster Social Skills:** Parents could encourage the child to interact with peers and participate in social activities. This can foster the child's social skills and empathy.

**Encourage Emotional Intelligence:** Parents can help the child to recognize and communicate their feelings and emotions in a constructive way. This can help reduce aggressive behavior and improve mental health.

**Provide Positive Reinforcement:** Instead of focusing solely on punishment, parents could use positive reinforcement to encourage good behavior.

**Show Unconditional Love:** Parents should ensure that their child knows they are loved unconditionally, regardless of their achievements or behavior.

Remember, every child is unique, and what works for one might not work for another. Parents should change their parenting methods based on the different needs of each child. It's also important to note that parenting is a journey, and it's okay to make mistakes along the way. The key is to learn from these mistakes and continue to strive to be the best parent you can be.

# A BALANCED PARENT AND BALANCED CHILD

## LETTER FROM A FOUR-YEAR-OLD TO A PREVIOUSLY AUTHORITARIAN BUT NOW BALANCED DAD

Dear Daddy,

Please, I remember when you used to always give me the biggest piece of cake. But now, you let me share it with my friends, and that's so fun! I feel like a big kid sharing like you. And now, we bake more cookies together too. You make the yummiest cookies, and I learn so much. It's my favorite time with you.

You're the best daddy in the whole wide world!

Love and cookie crumbs,

Your Little One

## RESPONSE FROM A PREVIOUSLY AUTHORITARIAN BUT NOW BALANCED DAD

Dear Little One,

Your letter made my day! I'm proud of you for wanting to learn about sharing. It's an important part of life, and I'm glad you're ready to learn. Please, we can definitely bake more cookies together. I enjoy our baking time too, and I'm glad to hear it's your favorite.

Thank you for your kind words. You're the best son a daddy could ever wish for!

Love and cookie crumbs back,

  Daddy

### LETTER FROM A FOUR-YEAR-OLD TO A PREVIOUSLY AUTHORITARIAN BUT NOW BALANCED MOM

Dear Mommy,

Please, I remember when we used to blow bubbles, and I would spill the soap. But now, you help me hold the wand carefully, and that's so fun! I feel like a big kid being careful like you. And now, we read more animal stories together too. You make the stories so fun, and I learn lots. It's my best time with you. You're the best mommy ever!

Hugs and bubbles,

Your Little One

### RESPONSE FROM A PREVIOUSLY AUTHORITARIAN BUT NOW BALANCED MOM

Dear Little One,

Your letter made my heart dance! I'm so proud of you for wanting to learn to be careful. That's a big part of blowing bubbles, and I'm happy you want to try. Please, we can definitely read more animal stories together. I love our story time too, and I'm thrilled it's your favorite.

Thank you for your sweet words. You're the most wonderful [son/daughter] a mommy could ever dream of!

Hugs and bubbles back,

Mommy

# PERMISSIVE PARENT

Permissive Parent: A permissive parent is like a fun-loving friend who lets you do whatever you want. They don't like to say 'no' and want you to have lots of fun, just like a friend would on a playdate.

## LETTER TO A PERMISSIVE DAD

Dear Daddy,

Please, I love it when we play with my toy planes! You always let me fly them so high, and that's so fun. But I heard Mommy saying that it's good to learn to put them back in the box too. Please could we please try that? I want to be neat and tidy like you.

And Daddy, please could we please read more airplane stories together? You make the stories so adventurous, and I learn a lot. It's my best time with you.

You're the best daddy ever!

Airplane sounds and storybooks,

Little One

## RESPONSE FROM A PERMISSIVE DAD

Dear Little One,

Your letter made me very happy! I'm glad you enjoy playing with your toy planes. It's important to put things away when we're done, and I'm always here to help you do that. Could we please read more airplane stories together? I enjoy our story time too, and I'm glad it's your favorite.

Thank you for your kind words. You're my little champ!

Airplane sounds and storybooks back,

Daddy

## LETTER TO A PERMISSIVE MOM

Dear Mommy,

Please, I love it when we play with my teddy bears! You always let me give them the biggest hugs, and that's so fun. But I heard Daddy saying that it's good to learn to put them back on the shelf too. Could we please try that? I want to be neat and tidy like you.

And Mommy, please could we please read more teddy bear stories together? You make the stories so cuddly, and I learn lots. It's my best time with you.

You're the best mommy ever!

Teddy bear hugs and storybooks,

Little One

## RESPONSE FROM A PERMISSIVE MOM

Dear Little One,

Your letter made me very happy! I'm glad you enjoy playing with your teddy bears. It's important to put things away when we're done, and I'm always here to help you do that. Could we please read more bible stories together?

I enjoyed the one about Noah very much, and I'm sure you will like it too. Thank you for your kind words. You're my little bundle of joy!

Teddy bear hugs and storybooks back,

Mommy

## LETTER TO A PERMISSIVE DAD

Dear Daddy,

I love it when we play with my toy we trucks! You always let me be the driver, and that's super fun. But Daddy says we should put the fire trucks away too. Please could we please do that next time? I want to be neat and tidy like you.

And Daddy, please could we please read more fire truck stories together? You make the stories so exciting, and I learn a lot. It's my best time with you.

You're the best daddy ever!

Train whistles and storybooks,

Little One

## RESPONSE FROM A PERMISSIVE DAD

Dear Little One,

Your letter made me very happy! I'm glad you enjoy playing with your toy fire trucks. It's important to put things away when we're done, and I'm always here to help you do that. Please then let us try to read more fire truck stories together. I enjoy our story time too, and I'm glad it's your favorite.

Thank you for your kind words. You're my little star!

Train whistles and storybooks back,

Daddy

## LETTER TO A PERMISSIVE MOM

Dear Mommy,

I love it when we play with my toy trucks! You always let me make the loudest vroom sounds, and that's super fun. But Daddy says we should put the trucks away too. Could we please do that next time? I want to be neat and tidy like you.

And Mommy, could we please read more truck stories together? You make the stories so exciting, and I learn lots. It's my best time with you.

You're the best mommy ever!

Truck sounds and storybooks,

Little One

## RESPONSE FROM A PERMISSIVE MOM

Dear Little One,

Your letter made me very happy! I'm glad you enjoy playing with your toy trucks. It's important to put things away when we're done, and I'm always here to help you do that. Could we please read more truck stories together? I enjoy our story time too, and I'm glad it's your favorite.

Thank you for your kind words. You're my little ray of sunshine!

Truck sounds and storybooks back,

Mommy

# LETTER TO A PERMISSIVE DAD

Dear Daddy,

I love it when we play with my toy boats! You always let me sail them so far, and that's super fun. But Daddy says we should put the boats away too. Could we please do that next time? I want to be neat and tidy like you.

And Daddy, could we please read more boat stories together? You make the stories so fun, and I learn a lot. It's my best time with you.

You're the best daddy ever!

Boat waves and storybooks,

Little One

# RESPONSE FROM A PERMISSIVE DAD

Dear Little One,

Your letter made me very happy! I'm glad you enjoy playing with your toy boats. It's important to put things away when we're done, and I'm always here to help you do that. Could we please read more boat stories together? I enjoy our story time too, and I'm glad it's your favorite.

Thank you for your kind words. You're my little adventurer!

Boat waves and storybooks back,

Daddy

## LETTER TO A PERMISSIVE MOM

Dear Mommy,

I love it when we play with my toy dolls! You always let me dress them up, and that's so fun. But I heard Daddy saying that it's good to learn to put them back in the dollhouse too. Could we please do that next time? I want to be neat and tidy like you. And Mommy, could we please read more doll stories together?

You make the stories so lovely, and I learn lots. It's my best time with you. You're the best mommy ever!

Doll dresses and storybooks,

Little One

## RESPONSE FROM A PERMISSIVE MOM

Dear Little One,

Your letter made my heart flutter! I'm glad you enjoy playing with your toy dolls. It's important to put things away when we're done, and I'm always here to help you do that. Yes, please, we can definitely read more doll stories together.

I enjoy our story time, too, and I'm glad it's your favorite. Thank you for your kind words. You're my little angel!

Doll dresses and storybooks back,

Mommy

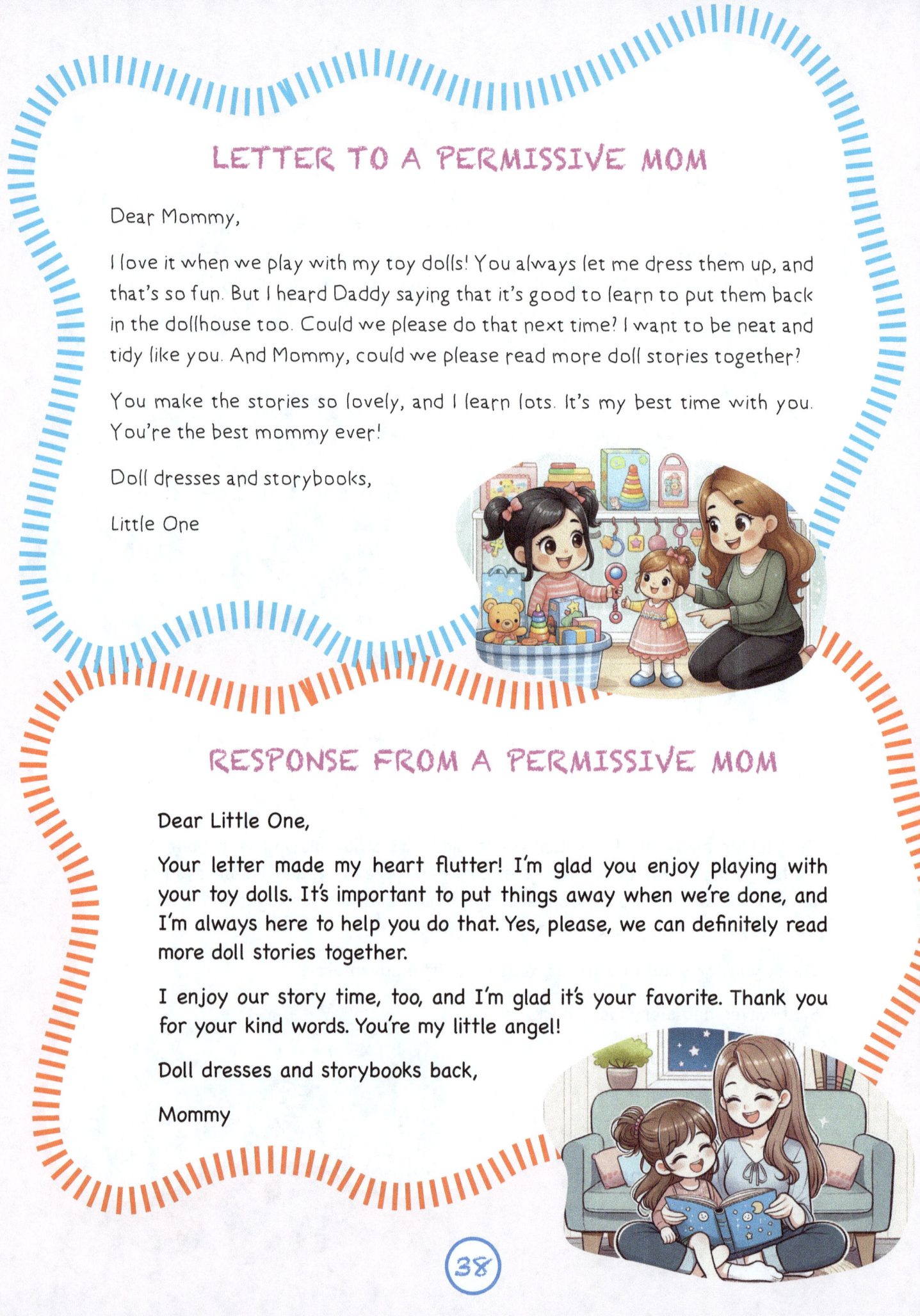

# BALANCED VS. UNBALANCED PARENTING: CONTRASTING CHILD OUTCOMES

Children raised by Permissive parents, like the ones described in the letters, may exhibit the following characteristics in society.

## POSITIVE OUTCOMES

**Parental Warmth:** Permissive parents are often warm and nurturing, which can lead to a close parent-child relationship.

**Self-Assurance:** Children are encouraged to express themselves freely, which can lead to increased self-confidence.

**Increased Creativity:** With fewer rules and restrictions, children may have the freedom to explore and become more creative.

**Protective Effects:** Studies have shown a connection between permissive parenting and averting risky behavior, including as substance abuse.

## NEGATIVE OUTCOMES

**Lack of Self-Discipline:** Children raised by permissive parents often lack self-discipline.

**Poor Social Skills:** These children may possess poor social skills.

**Self-Centeredness:** They may be self-involved and demanding.

**Insecurity:** They may feel insecure due to the lack of boundaries and guidance.

**Risk-Prone Temperament:** When children lack appropriate boundaries, they have to care for themselves and may approach certain circumstances without hesitation or fear. This can increase their propensity to engage in dangerous behavior, such as drug use.

**Rebellion:** They may rebel against rules and expectations.

**Unhealthy Habits:** They may develop unhealthy habits.

**Poor Academic Performance:** Permissive parenting is often linked to poor academic performance.

To balance the child's outcomes and ensure they grow up to be wonderful and beneficial to humanity and society, parents practicing a permissive parenting style could consider incorporating elements of the authoritative parenting style. Here are some steps they can take:

**Set Clear Boundaries:** Permissive parents often lack clear boundaries. Instead, they could set clear and consistent rules and expectations. This can help the child develop self-discipline and feel more secure.

**Promote Responsibility:** Rather than allowing the children to do whatever they want, parents could gradually give their children more responsibility and encourage them to make their own decisions. This helps the child develop independence and confidence.

**Teach Social Skills:** Parents could encourage the child to interact with peers and participate in social activities. This can enhance the child's social abilities and compassion.

**Promote Healthy Behaviors:** Parents could demonstrate and foster healthy behaviors, such as a nutritious diet and consistent exercise. This can help prevent the development of unhealthy habits.

**Promote Academic Success:** Parents could set high expectations for academic performance and provide support and resources to help the child succeed.

**Teach Respect for Others:** Parents should model respect for others and teach their children to do the same. This helps the child develop empathy and reduces self-centeredness.

**Teach Coping Mechanisms:** Parents should teach their children how to cope with failure and disappointment. This can help reduce insecurity and improve resilience.

**Encourage Safe Risk-Taking:** Parents should encourage their children to take risks and explore new things in a safe and supportive environment. This can help the child learn to navigate the world, make decisions, and become more independent.

Remember, every child is unique and what works for one might not work for another. Parents should adjust their parenting approaches to suit the specific needs of their children. It's also important to note that parenting is a journey, and it's okay to make mistakes along the way. The key is to learn from these mistakes and continue to strive to be the best parent you can be.

# A BALANCED PARENT AND BALANCED CHILD

### LETTER FROM A FOUR-YEAR-OLD TO A PREVIOUSLY PERMISSIVE BUT NOW BALANCED DAD

Dear Daddy,

Please remember when we used to play with my toy planes all day and leave them everywhere. But now, we put them back in the box after playing, and I like that! It's fun to be neat and tidy like you. And now, please read more airplane stories together. You make the stories so adventurous, and I learn lots. It's my best time with you. You're the best daddy ever!

Airplane sounds and storybooks,

Little One

### RESPONSE FROM A PREVIOUSLY PERMISSIVE BUT NOW BALANCED DAD

Dear Little One,

Your letter made me very happy! I'm glad you enjoy playing with your toy planes and putting them away after. Please, it's important to be neat and tidy. I also enjoy our airplane story time, and I'm glad it's your favorite. Thank you for your kind words. You're my little champ!

Airplane sounds and storybooks back,

Daddy

## LETTER FROM A FOUR-YEAR-OLD TO A PREVIOUSLY PERMISSIVE BUT NOW BALANCED MOM

Dear Mommy,

Please remember when we used to play with my teddy bears all day and leave them all over the place. But now, we put them back on the shelf after playing, and I like that! It's fun to be neat and tidy like you. And now, please we, read more teddy bear stories together. You make the stories so cuddly, and I learn lots. It's my best time with you. You're the best mommy ever!

Teddy bear hugs and storybooks,

Little One

## RESPONSE FROM A PREVIOUSLY PERMISSIVE BUT NOW BALANCED MOM

Dear Little One,

Your letter made my heart flutter! I'm glad you enjoy playing with your teddy bears and putting them away after. It's important to be neat and tidy. Please, I also enjoy our teddy bear story time, and I'm glad it's your favorite. Thank you for your kind words. You're my little bundle of joy!

Teddy bear hugs and storybooks back,

Mommy

# UNINVOLVED PARENT

Uninvolved Parent: An uninvolved parent is like a big tree in a park. The tree is always there, but it doesn't play with you or talk to you. You can play around the tree and have fun on your own, but the tree doesn't help you or give you hugs.

Sometimes, you might wish the tree could be more like a friend who listens to you and helps you when you need it.

## LETTER TO AN UNINVOLVED DAD

Dear Daddy,

Please, can I play with my toys alone? I promise to be good and not make a mess. I'll call you if I need help.

Love and giggles,

Little Son

## RESPONSE FROM AN UNINVOLVED DAD

Dear Little Son,

Of course, champ. Please enjoy playing with your toys. Remember to clean up after you're done. Have fun!

Love and high fives,

Daddy

## LETTER TO AN UNINVOLVED MOM

Dear Mommy,

Can I please color my coloring book by myself? I'll be careful not to color outside the lines. I'll call you if I need help.

Hugs and kisses,

Little One

## RESPONSE FROM AN UNINVOLVED MOM

Dear Little One,

Absolutely, sweetheart. Please enjoy coloring your book. Remember to put the colors back in the box when you're done. Have fun!

Hugs and kisses,

Mommy

## LETTER TO AN UNINVOLVED DAD

Dear Daddy,

Can I please watch my favorite cartoon? I'll sit quietly and won't change the channel. I'll call you if I need anything.

Love and giggles,

Little Daughter

## RESPONSE FROM AN UNINVOLVED DAD

Dear Little Daughter,

Sure, princess. Please enjoy your cartoon. Remember, only one episode. Have fun!

Love and fairy dust,

Daddy

### LETTER TO AN UNINVOLVED MOM

Dear Mommy,

Can I please watch my favorite show on TV? I'll sit quietly and won't turn up the volume too high. I'll call you if I need anything.

Hugs and kisses,

Little One

### RESPONSE FROM AN UNINVOLVED MOM

Dear Little One,

Sure, darling. Please, enjoy your show. Remember, only one episode. Have fun!

Hugs and kisses,

Mommy

## LETTER TO AN UNINVOLVED DAD

Dear Daddy,

Please, can I go to play in the garden? I'll stay where you can see me and won't go near the road. I'll call you if I need anything.

Love and giggles,

Little Son

## RESPONSE FROM AN UNINVOLVED DAD

Dear Little Son,

Absolutely, my little explorer. Please, have fun playing in the garden. Remember to stay safe and call me if you need anything.

Love and high fives,

Daddy

## LETTER TO AN UNINVOLVED MOM

Dear Mommy,

Can I please play with my blocks in my room? I'll build a big tower and won't leave blocks on the floor. I'll call you if I need anything.

Hugs and kisses,

Your Little Girl

## RESPONSE FROM AN UNINVOLVED MOM

Dear Your Little Girl,

Of course, my little builder. Please have fun building your tower. Remember to pick up all the blocks when you're done.

Hugs and kisses,

Mommy

# BALANCED VS. UNBALANCED PARENTING: CONTRASTING CHILD OUTCOMES

Children raised by uninvolved parents can experience both positive and negative outcomes. Here are some potential outcomes:

## POSITIVE OUTCOMES

**Independence:** Children may learn to be self-reliant and independent at an early age. They might develop problem-solving skills as they navigate situations on their own.

**Resilience:** These children might become resilient and adaptable, learning to cope with challenges without much parental intervention.

**Creativity:** Children could be more creative if they have more space to pursue their passions and discover their talents without parents supervising them.

## NEGATIVE OUTCOMES

**Low Self-Esteem:** Children might feel neglected or unimportant, leading to low self-esteem and confidence.

**Poor Social Skills:** Without parental guidance, children might struggle to develop appropriate social skills and have difficulty forming healthy relationships.

**Behavioral Problems:** Children might exhibit behavioral problems, such as defiance or aggression, as a way to seek attention or express their feelings of neglect.

It is important to note that these are potential outcomes and can vary greatly depending on the child's personality, resilience, and other environmental factors. It's always best for parents to provide a balance of independence and guidance to support their child's development. Keep in mind that each child is special and may react differently to different parenting approaches. It's always best to choose a style that best suits the child's needs and personality.

To balance the child's outcomes and ensure they grow up to be wonderful and beneficial to humanity and society, parents practicing an uninvolved parenting style could consider incorporating elements of the authoritative parenting style. Here are some steps they can take:

**Show Interest and Involvement:** Uninvolved parents often lack involvement in their children's lives. Instead, they could show interest in their children's activities, feelings, and experiences. This can help the child feel valued and understood.

**Set Clear Boundaries:** Uninvolved parents often lack clear boundaries. Instead, they could set clear and consistent rules and expectations. This can help the child develop self-discipline and feel more secure.

**Promote Responsibility:** Rather than allowing the children to do whatever they want, parents could gradually give their children more responsibility and encourage them to make their own decisions. This helps the child develop independence and confidence.

**Teach Social Skills:** Parents could encourage the child to interact with peers and participate in social activities. This can foster the child's social abilities and compassion.

**Promote Healthy Behaviors:** Parents could demonstrate and foster healthy behaviors, such as a nutritious diet and frequent exercise. This can help prevent the development of unhealthy habits.

**Provide Emotional Support:** Parents should provide emotional support and love, showing their children that they'll be there for them, no matter what.

Remember, every child is unique, and what works for one might not work for another. Parents should adjust their parenting methods to suit the specific needs of their children. It's also important to note that parenting is a journey, and it's okay to make mistakes along the way. The key is to learn from these mistakes and continue to strive to be the best parent you can be.

# A BALANCED PARENT AND BALANCED CHILD

### LETTER FROM A FOUR-YEAR-OLD TO A PREVIOUSLY UNINVOLVED BUT NOW BALANCED DAD

Dear Daddy,

Please, I remember when I used to play by myself a lot, but now we play together so much, and I love it! You always make time for me now, and that makes me feel so happy. I like it when you help me build towers with my blocks, but please I also like it when you let me play by myself sometimes.

Please, I know you're always there if I need help, and that makes me feel safe. I love you more than all the stars in the sky. You're the best daddy in the whole wide world!

Love and giggles,

[Your Little One's Name

### RESPONSE FROM A PREVIOUSLY UNINVOLVED BUT NOW BALANCED DAD

Dear Little One,

Your letter warms my heart! I'm so glad to hear that you're happy. I love spending time with you, whether we're playing together or you're playing by yourself.

Please remember, I'm always here for you, no matter what. Your love means more to me than all the stars in the sky. You're the best [son/daughter] a daddy could ever ask for!

Love and high fives,

Daddy

### LETTER FROM A FOUR-YEAR-OLD TO A PREVIOUSLY UNINVOLVED BUT NOW BALANCED MOM

Dear Mommy,

Please remember when I used to read by myself a lot, but now we read stories together, and it's super fun! You make the characters come alive. I also like it when you let me read by myself sometimes.

You always know just what to do when I feel yucky. You kiss my boo-boos and make them better. I love you more than all the toys in the world. You're the best mommy ever!

Big hugs and kisses,

Your Little One

### RESPONSE FROM A PREVIOUSLY UNINVOLVED BUT NOW BALANCED MOM

Dear Little One,

Your letter fills my heart with joy! I'm so glad to hear that you enjoy our story times. I love reading to you, and I'm proud of you for reading by yourself too.

Please remember, I'm always here to make you feel better when you're feeling yucky. Your love means more to me than all the toys in the world. You're the best [son/daughter] a mommy could ever ask for!

Big hugs and kisses back,

Mommy

# SAYING NO TO A CHILD

## A CHILD'S REQUEST

Dear Mommy and Daddy,

Can we go to a place with snow and mountains? I saw a picture of it. I want to learn to ski and make a snowman with you. I think it would be so cool!

We can drink hot cocoa and sit by the fire. I'll wear my warmest coat and gloves, I promise. Can we please plan a trip to the snow? It would be so much fun!

Love and snowflakes,

Little Son

## DAD'S "COMPASSIONATE REFUSAL"

Dear Little Son,

Your letter warmed our hearts! We know how much you want to go to the snowy mountains. It sounds like a great adventure!

But right now, we need to save our money for other important things. Going on a vacation to the mountains costs a lot of money for the stay, the food, and the travel.

We promise that we will try our best to take you there one day when we can. Until then, we can have fun in many other ways at home and nearby!

Love and hugs,

Mommy and Daddy

### A CHILD'S REQUEST

Dear Mommy,

Can we please go to the park now? I really want to play on the swings and slide.

Love,

Little One

### MOM'S "EMPATHETIC DENIAL"

Dear Little One,

I know how much you love the park and playing on the swings and slides. However, it's raining outside right now. We can't go out in the rain because we might catch a cold. But don't worry, we can play with your favorite board game inside instead. We'll go to the park as soon as the weather gets better, I promise.

Love,

Mommy

### A CHILD'S REQUEST

Dear Daddy,

Can I please stay up late tonight to watch the new cartoon movie?

Love,

Little One

### DAD'S "COMPASSIONATE REFUSAL"

Dear Little One,

I understand that you're excited about the new cartoon movie. However, it's important to get enough sleep, especially on school nights. How about we watch the movie together this weekend instead?

Love,

Dad

### A CHILD'S REQUEST

Dear Mommy,

Can I please have ice cream before dinner? I promise to still eat my dinner.

Love,

Little One

### MOM'S "EMPATHETIC DENIAL"

Dear Little One,

My little one, I understand that you love ice cream. However, it's important that we eat our dinner first. Eating ice cream before could spoil your appetite for the yummy dinner we're going to have. But don't worry, you can have some ice cream after dinner as a treat!

Love,

Mommy

### A CHILD'S REQUEST

Dear Dad,

Please, can we get a puppy? I promise to take care of it and play with it every day.

Love,

Little One

### DAD'S "COMPASSIONATE REFUSAL"

Dear Little One,

Please, I know how much you love puppies and how much you would like to have one. However, puppies need a lot of care and attention, just like little children. Right now, we might not have enough time to properly take care of a puppy. But we can visit the animal shelter and spend some time with the puppies there. And who knows, maybe in the future, we might be able to get a puppy.

Love,

Dady

### A CHILD'S REQUEST

Dear Mommy,

Can we please invite my friend from school for a sleepover? We can watch cartoons and eat cookies.

Love,

Little Daughter

### MOM'S "EMPATHETIC DENIAL"

Dear Little Daughter,

I know how much fun sleepovers can be and how much you enjoy spending time with your friends. However, right now, we need to make sure we're keeping everyone safe and healthy, and that means not having sleepovers for a little while. But don't worry, you can still video call your friend and watch cartoons together online. And we can definitely make some cookies for that!

Love,

Mommy

### A CHILD'S REQUEST

Dear Mom,

Can we please go to the toy store? I want to buy a new toy with my allowance.

Love,

Little Son

### MOM'S "EMPATHETIC DENIAL"

Dear Little Son,

I understand that you're excited to buy a new toy with your allowance. However, right now, we need to stay home to keep everyone safe and healthy. But don't worry, we can look at toys online, and you can choose one to buy with your allowance.

Love,

Mom

## A CHILD'S REQUEST

Dear Daddy,

Can we please go fishing this weekend? I want to learn how to catch fish. I promise to be patient and quiet.

We can bring sandwiches and juice for a picnic. It will be a fun adventure! Can we please do that?

Love and hugs,

Little Son

## DAD'S "COMPASSIONATE REFUSAL"

Dear Little Son,

Your letter made me smile! I love your enthusiasm for learning new things. Fishing does require patience and quiet, and I'm glad you're ready for it.

However, this weekend, we plan to visit Grandma. But don't worry, we can plan our fishing trip for next weekend. We'll pack sandwiches and juice for a picnic, just like you suggested.

Thank you for being so understanding. I'm looking forward to our fishing adventure.

Love and hugs back,

Daddy

## A CHILD'S REQUEST

Dear Daddy,

Can we please build a treehouse in the backyard? I want to have a secret place where I can read my comic books. I promise to help with the building and cleaning.

We can paint it green and blue. It will be our special project! Can we please do that?

Love and high fives,

Your Little Daughter

## DAD'S "COMPASSIONATE REFUSAL"

Dear Little Daughter,

Your letter filled my heart with joy! Building a treehouse sounds like a great project. However, building a treehouse is a big task and requires a lot of time and materials.

Right now, we might not have all the things we need. But we can start by making a plan and gathering the materials little by little. How does that sound?

Thank you for being so excited about our projects. I'm sure we'll have a lot of fun planning and building together.

Love and high fives back,

Daddy

# 6 | EFFECTIVELY PUNISHING A CHILD

### POSITIVE PUNISHMENT FROM DAD

Dear Little One,

I noticed that you took a cookie from the jar even after I told you not to. It's important to listen when Daddy says no. It's not because I want to be mean, but because eating too many sweets is not good for your teeth.

As a result, you will have to brush your teeth an extra time today. I hope you understand why this is necessary.

Love,

Daddy

### RESPONSE FROM THE CHILD

Dear Daddy,

I'm sorry for taking the cookie. I understand now that it's not good for my teeth. I will listen next time when you say no.

Love,

Your Little One

## POSITIVE PUNISHMENT FROM MOM

Dear Little One,

I saw that you didn't clean up your toys after playing, even though I asked you to. It's important to keep our home tidy. If we leave toys around, someone might trip and get hurt. Because of this, you will have to spend some extra time tidying up today. I hope you understand why this is important.

Love,

Mommy

## RESPONSE FROM THE CHILD

Dear Mommy,

I'm sorry for not cleaning up my toys. I understand now that someone might get hurt. I will remember to clean up next time.

Love,

Your Little One

## POSITIVE PUNISHMENT FROM DAD

Dear Little One,

I noticed that you were not nice to your sister today. It's important to treat everyone with kindness. When we say mean things, it can hurt other people's feelings. Because of this, you will have to spend some time today thinking about how to make it up to her. I hope you understand why this is important.

Love,

Daddy

## RESPONSE FROM THE CHILD

Dear Daddy,

I'm sorry for not being nice to my sister. I understand now that it's important to be kind. I will think about how to make it up to her.

Love,

Your Little One

## POSITIVE PUNISHMENT FROM MOM

Dear Little One,

I saw that you were not sharing your toys with your sister today. Sharing is important because it shows we care about others. Because of this, you will have to let your sister choose the games you play together tomorrow. I hope you understand why this is necessary.

Love,

Mom

## RESPONSE FROM THE CHILD

Dear Mommy,

I'm sorry for not sharing my toys. I understand now that it's important to show we care. I will remember to share next time.

Love,

Your Little One

## POSITIVE PUNISHMENT FROM DAD

Dear Little One,

I noticed that you didn't clean up your room after playing, even though I asked you to. Keeping our spaces tidy is important because it helps us stay organized and take care of our things. Because of this, you will have to spend some extra time cleaning your room tomorrow. I hope you understand why this is necessary.

Love,

Dad

## RESPONSE FROM THE CHILD

Dear Daddy,

I'm sorry for not cleaning up my room. I understand now that it's important to stay organized. I will remember to clean up next time.

Love,

Your Little One

## POSITIVE PUNISHMENT FROM MOM

Dear Little One,

Today, you were not being nice to your friend at the park. Being kind to others is important because it shows respect and makes others feel good. Because of this, you will have to apologize to your friends and think of a way to make it up to them. I hope you understand why this is necessary.

Love,

Mom

## RESPONSE FROM THE CHILD

Dear Mom,

I'm sorry for not being nice to my friend. I understand now that it's important to show respect. I will remember to be kind next time.

Love,

Little One

## POSITIVE PUNISHMENT FROM DAD

Dear Little One,

You didn't finish your homework before playing video games today. Completing our responsibilities before fun activities is important because it helps us stay on track and succeed. Because of this, you will have to do some extra homework tomorrow. I hope you understand why this is necessary.

Love,

Dad

## RESPONSE FROM THE CHILD

Dear Daddy,

I'm sorry for not finishing my homework. I understand now that it's important to complete my responsibilities. I will remember to finish my homework before playing next time.

Love,

Your Little One

## POSITIVE PUNISHMENT FROM MOM

Dear Little One,

You didn't brush your teeth before bed tonight. Taking care of our health is important because it helps us stay strong and healthy. Because of this, you will have to brush your teeth an extra time tomorrow. I hope you understand why this is necessary.

Love,

Mom

## RESPONSE FROM THE CHILD

Dear Mommy,

I'm sorry for not brushing my teeth. I understand now that it's important to take care of my health. I will remember to brush my teeth before bed next time.

Love,

Your Little One

## NEGATIVE YET EFFECTIVE PUNISHMENT FROM DAD

Dear Little One,

I noticed that you took a candy from the jar even after I told you not to. It's important to listen when Daddy says no. It's not because I want to be mean, but because eating too many sweets is not good for your teeth.

As a result, you will have to brush your teeth an extra time today. I hope you understand why this is necessary.

Love,

Daddy

## RESPONSE FROM THE CHILD

Dear Daddy,

I'm sorry for taking the candy. I understand now that it's not good for my teeth. I will listen next time when you say no.

Love,

Your Little One

## NEGATIVE YET EFFECTIVE PUNISHMENT FROM MOM

Dear Little One,

I saw that you didn't clean up your toys after playing, even though I asked you to. It's important to keep our home tidy. If we leave toys around, someone might trip and get hurt.

Because of this, you won't be able to play with your toys for the rest of the day. I hope you understand why this is important.

Love,

Mommy

## RESPONSE FROM THE CHILD

Dear Mommy,

I'm sorry for not cleaning up my toys. I understand now that someone might get hurt. I will remember to clean up next time.

Love,

Your Little One

## NEGATIVE YET EFFECTIVE PUNISHMENT FROM DAD

Dear Little One,

I noticed that you were not nice to your sister today. It's important to treat everyone with kindness. When we say mean things, it can hurt other people's feelings.

Because of this, you won't be able to play your video game today. I hope you understand why this is important.

Love,

Daddy

## RESPONSE FROM THE CHILD

Dear Daddy,

Please, I'm really sorry for not being nice to my sister. I didn't mean to hurt her feelings. I understand now that it's important to be kind to everyone. I promise I will try to be nicer to her from now on. Please I understand why I can't play my video game today, and I will remember this lesson.

Love,

Your Little One

## NEGATIVE YET EFFECTIVE PUNISHMENT FROM DAD

Dear Little One,

I saw that you were not sharing your toys with your sister today. Please sharing is important because it shows we care about others.

Because of this, you won't be able to play with your toys for the rest of the day. Please, I hope you understand why this is necessary.

Love,

Daddy

## RESPONSE FROM THE CHILD

Dear Daddy,

Please, I'm sorry for not sharing my toys. Please, I understand now that it's important to show we care. I will remember to share next time.

Love,

Your Little One

## NEGATIVE YET EFFECTIVE PUNISHMENT FROM MOM

Dear Little One,

I noticed that you didn't clean up your room after playing, even though I asked you to. Keeping our spaces tidy is important because it helps us stay organized and take care of our things.

Because of this, you won't be able to watch your favorite TV show today. Please, I hope you understand why this is necessary.

Love,

Mommy

## RESPONSE FROM THE CHILD

Dear Mommy,

Please, I'm sorry for not cleaning up my room. Please understand now that it's important to stay organized. I will remember to clean up next time.

Love,

Your Little One

## NEGATIVE YET EFFECTIVE PUNISHMENT FROM DAD

Dear Little One,

Today, you were not being nice to your friend at the park. Please to be kind to others is important because it shows respect and makes others feel good.

Because of this, you won't be able to go to the park tomorrow. Please, I hope you understand why this is necessary.

Love,

Daddy

## RESPONSE FROM THE CHILD

Dear Daddy,

Please, I'm sorry for not being nice to my friend. Please understand now that it's important to show respect. Please I will remember to be kind next time.

Love,

Your Little One

## NEGATIVE YET EFFECTIVE PUNISHMENT FROM MOM

Dear Little One,

Please I notice that you didn't finish your homework before playing video games today. Completing our responsibilities before fun activities is important because it helps us stay on track and succeed.

Because of this, you won't be able to play video games tomorrow. Please, I hope you understand why this is necessary.

Love,

Mommy

## RESPONSE FROM THE CHILD

Dear Mommy,

Please, I'm sorry for not finishing my homework. I understand now that it's important to complete my responsibilities. Please I will remember to finish my homework before playing next time.

Love,

Your Little One

### NEGATIVE YET EFFECTIVE PUNISHMENT FROM DAD

Dear Little One,

Please I notice that you didn't brush your teeth before bed tonight. Taking care of our health is important because it helps us stay strong and healthy.

Because of this, you won't be able to have dessert tomorrow. Please, I hope you understand why this is necessary.

Love,

Daddy

### RESPONSE FROM THE CHILD

Dear Daddy,

Please, I'm sorry for not brushing my teeth. I understand now that it's important to take care of my health. Please I will remember to brush my teeth before bed next time.

Love,

Your Little One

# CONCLUSION

As we reach the end of this collection, I hope these letters have provided you with a deeper understanding of the impact of parenting styles on children. These preschoolers' words remind us that every interaction we have with our children shapes their world. May this book inspire you to reflect on your own parenting style and make the necessary adjustments to foster a nurturing and supportive environment for your child.

# ACKNOWLEDGMENTS

I am profoundly grateful to everyone who gave me the opportunity to finish this book. I give special gratitude to our children whose letters not only formed the backbone of this work but also served as a source of inspiration. Their honesty and innocence are truly inspiring.

I am extremely grateful to all parents who strive to understand and connect with their children on a deeper level. Your dedication and love are the essence of this book.

I would also like to extend my thanks to the readers for embarking on this journey of understanding and growth with us. Your engagement and feedback are invaluable in making this work a valuable resource for parents everywhere.

Lastly, I would like to thank everyone who has been a part of this project. Your support and encouragement were, in the end, what made this book possible.

Thank you for taking the time to engage with this work. Your contributions are greatly appreciated.

# WELCOME TO OUR PARACLETE FAMILY!!

Ewuramma Hannah Boah, the author of five other books on Family, marriage, and the Holy Spirit presents this book as a testament to the profound impact of parenting styles on a child's development. This book, a collection of heartfelt letters from preschoolers to their parents, provides a unique insight into their world. It serves as a window into the innocent minds of children, revealing their emotions, feelings, and perceptions of their parents' styles.

The Paraclete Family is dedicated to providing inspiration, comfort, advocacy, guidance, knowledge, and godly advice to people in all phases of life, especially children. We urge every parent to extend their parenting not only to their own children but also to other children who lack parental guidance. We encourage parents to be empathetic, loving yet authoritative, and to interact cheerfully and supportively with children, especially those experiencing a lack of parenting.

We should be vigilant for the millions of children we encounter daily, consoling and loving them with tender remarks. We should also salute them with heartfelt encouragement and offer our strength for their support and safety. This is precisely what Christians do and what the Paraclete Family stands for.

Whether you received this book as a gift, borrowed it, or purchased it yourself, we are glad you read it. It is just one of the many helpful, insightful, and encouraging resources produced by our Paraclete Family. Thank you for taking the time to engage with this work. Your feedback and criticism are welcome, as they provide opportunities for growth and improvement. This book is for you.

In conclusion, let us remember that children are gifts from God, and we should treat them as such. As it is written in Psalm 127:3, NLT: "Children are a gift from the LORD; they are a reward from him."

May our Paraclete, the Third Person of the Blessed Trinity, enlighten us so that we recognize we are one Family united by love. May He bless us so that we can bless everyone that comes our way. Amen!

## EMAIL US YOUR STORY!!!

We warmly invite you to share your experiences and insights on how the conversations in "Tiny Hearts With Big Feelings" have impacted your life, whether as a child, parent, sibling, teacher, or someone you know. Your feedback is invaluable to us. Please feel free to reach out to Ewuramma at ourparacletefoundation.inc@gmail.com.

Our Paraclete Foundation Inc. is a non-profit organization dedicated to reminding everyone that they are cherished by God. Our mission is to ensure that every individual realizes and feels the unconditional love that God has for us. We believe that this understanding will naturally lead us to reciprocate His love.

As our knowledge of divine love grows, our faith strengthens, and our commitment to parenting our children rightly and loving one another deepens. All these responsibilities, mutual love, and respect serve as a testament to the world that we are indeed one Family originating from one race.

We pray for God's grace to guide us so that the very essence of our being is compelled to surrender our hearts to God, fostering godly human relationships, marriages, and parenting. We believe that we can build a world through all our resources where responsibility, love, unity, and mutual respect are the norm. Thank you for being a part of this journey with us.

# BIBLIOGRAPHY

**Authoritative Parenting:** What Is It, Examples, Effects, and More. https://psychcentral.com/health/authoritative-parenting.

**Authoritative Parenting:** Characteristics and Effects - Verywell Mind. https://www.verywellmind.com/what-is-authoritative-parenting-2794956.

**Authoritative Parenting:** Balance Discipline And Love - Parenting For Brain. https://www.parentingforbrain.com/authoritative-parenting/.

**The authoritative parenting style:** An evidence-based guide. https://parentingscience.com/authoritative-parenting-style/.

**What is Authoritative Parenting?** | TalkingParents. https://talkingparents.com/parenting-resources/authoritative-parenting.

**Authoritarian Parenting:** Examples, Definition, Effects - Verywell Mind. https://www.verywellmind.com/what-is-authoritarian-parenting-2794955.

**Authoritarian Parenting:** Its Impact, Causes, and Indications. https://www.psychologytoday.com/us/blog/overcoming-destructive-anger/202402/authoritarian-parenting-its-impact-causes-and-indications.

**Authoritarian Parenting:** What Is It? - WebMD. https://www.webmd.com/parenting/authoritarian-parenting-what-is-it.

**Authoritarian Parenting:** Characteristics & Drawbacks - Choosing Therapy. https://www.choosingtherapy.com/authoritarian-parenting/.

**Uninvolved Parenting:** Examples, Characteristics, Effects - Verywell Mind. https://www.verywellmind.com/what-is-uninvolved-parenting-2794958.

**Uninvolved Parenting:** Pros and Cons, Effects, Examples, More - Healthline. https://www.healthline.com/health/parenting/uninvolved-parenting.

**Uninvolved Parenting:** Characteristics, Causes, Effects - Mindsight Clinic. https://mindsightclinic.com/blog/parenting/what-is-uninvolved-parenting/.

**Uninvolved Parenting:** Definition, Characteristics, & Impact. https://www.choosingtherapy.com/uninvolved-parenting/.

**Helicopter Parenting:** Examples, Causes, Effects. https://www.parents.com/parenting/better-parenting/what-is-helicopter-parenting/.

**Helicopter Parenting:** What It Is and Pros and Cons - Healthline. https://www.healthline.com/health/parenting/helicopter-parenting.

**Characteristics of Helicopter Parenting** - Parenting For Brain. https://www.parentingforbrain.com/helicopter-parents/.

**Helicopter Parenting:** How it Affects Your Child's Mental Health - WebMD. https://www.webmd.com/parenting/what-to-know-about-helicopter-parenting.

**What Is Permissive Parenting?** - Verywell Mind. https://www.verywellmind.com/what-is-permissive-parenting-2794957.

**Permissive Parenting Style:** Examples and Effects. https://www.parents.com/parenting/better-parenting/style/permissive-parenting-the-pros-and-cons-according-to-a-child-psychologist/.

**(What is Permissive Parenting?** How Does It Affect the Child?. https://www.choosingtherapy.com/permissive-parenting/.

**Understanding Permissive Parenting:** How It Affects Your Child's .... https://smartparentingpod.com/understanding-permissive-parenting-how-it-affects-your-childs-development/.

**Uninvolved Parenting:** Examples, Characteristics, Effects - Verywell Mind. https://www.verywellmind.com/what-is-uninvolved-parenting-2794958.

**Uninvolved Parenting:** Pros and Cons, Effects, Examples, More - Healthline. https://www.healthline.com/health/parenting/uninvolved-parenting.

**Uninvolved Parenting:** Characteristics, Causes, Effects - Mindsight Clinic. https://mindsightclinic.com/blog/parenting/what-is-uninvolved-parenting/.

**Uninvolved Parenting:** Definition, Characteristics, & Impact. https://www.choosingtherapy.com/uninvolved-parenting/.

www.ingramcontent.com/pod-product-compliance
Lightning Source LLC
Chambersburg PA
CBHW082246300426
44110CB00039B/2452